GO AHEAD LET GO!

MESHEL JOYCE POMMELLS, BBA

To order additional copies of this book, contact:
Xlibris
844-714-8691
www.Xlibris.com
Orders@Xlibris.com

ISBN: Softcover   978-1-4415-8902-6
        EBook   979-8-3694-1455-2

Library of Congress Control Number: 2009911242

Print information available on the last page

Rev. date: 01/08/2024

Philippians 4: 13

"I can do all things through Christ who give me strength".

Deuteronomy 6: 5

"Love the Lord your God with all your heart, soul and strength".

ACKNOWLEDGEMENT

I give honor to God who is the head of my life. Thanks for pre-destinated me for progress, for success and for prosperity. Thanks for all the blessings and all the wonderful gifts in my life.

Dedication

To all the members of Davyton United Church, Jamaica WI. Bethel Evangelical Church, Brooklyn, NY. and Love Gospel Assembly, Bronx, NY.,

For my mother **Rose**, who choose to carry me into this world, my father **Keith Pommells** and my beloved grandmother, Mrs. Lydia Williams. My two brothers, **Paul** and **O'Neil** and my four sisters, **Alice, Patrice, Avalone** and **Valeria**. All my nieces and nephews, cousins and family members too many to name. I love you all very much.

My four children:
Tiffani, my sweet charming first child, you are a gift and I love every minute you spend in my life. You were name after a famous "Tiffany's Jewelry store".

Tony (TJ) my only son, surrounded by a bunch of girls to help you grow strong, you have a common family name, if at a family re-union someone call, TONY" a lot of men would come running.

Tashel, my princess, you were the easiest to be born, your father held you the whole time after your birth, guess that is why you love him so much, **Tafari** and I made up your name when we were teenagers.

Rosemarie, you are a smart little girl, you came close to kicking the bucket at birth and you were named after your two grandmothers, your dad's mom is Rosemary and mine is Rose.

Mrs. **Lydia Williams** who is now with the lord, "mama", she raised me to serve the Lord, who waked us up every morning at 6 a.m., to pray and in the evening read the bible.

"Train up a child in the way he should grow and when he is old would not depart from it . . . .
KJV

LIFE WHERE WILL IT LEADS?

As we go through each day
Do you every stop to ponder?
Where am I going?
We do not have to pretend
Just really follow our deepest thoughts
The answer is always there
Just stop for a moment to listen.
Do not be dismayed
Each day has a new challenge
What will it be?
Flee or face it?
Life will always be
It was before we came on the scene
And it will continue after we are gone
Do not just exit
LIVE

By Meshel J. Pommells 2/02

Chapter 1

Holy Spirit = Boldness

"Now about spiritual gifts, brother I do not want you to be ignorant, you know that when you were influenced and led astray to mute idols".

"Therefore I tell you that no one who is speaking by the spirit of God says "Jesus be cursed" and no one can say "Jesus is Lord" except but the Holy Spirit".

"There are different kinds of gifts but the same spirit; there are different kinds of service but the same Lord". "There are difference kinds of working, but the same God works all of them in all men".

"Now to each one the manifestation of the spirit is given for the common good to one there is given through the spirit the message of wisdom, to another the message of knowledge by means of the same spirit to another faith by the same spirit to another miraculous powers to another prophecy".

"To another the distinguishing between spirits and to another speaking in different tongue"!

All these are the work of one and the same spirit and he gave then each one, just as he determines.

The body is a unit, through it is made up of many parts and though all its parts are many they form one body.

So it is with Christ for we were all baptized by one spirit into one body.

Whether Jews or Greeks slave or free and we were all given the spirit to drink from the fountain of life. (1 Cor. 12:1-18)

Reading and writing has always being a part of my joy and my gift, I realize that from my childhood, I would take papers and staple them together and made many diaries to write my thought or songs.

After reading several books, it came to me that I should also share my faith and view of the Holy God of Israel.

A Christian joke . . . The other day I read a story in my e-mail about a Rabbi, who was complaining that he sent his son to Israel and he came back a Christian, each Rabbi he spoke with also sent their sons to Israel and they also became Christians.

So, as he knelt down to pray to God and asked for his divine intervention. He heard a voice saying "I also send my son to Israel". (That is Jesus)

One of my many jobs landed me into Manhattan where I had an experience as I sat as a companion with a Jewish Youth, in the Rehabilitation building, **Burnstein**.

I had an experience one night in **Beth Israel Medical Center**, there in the hospital, which housed rehabilitation residents. I was in aught as I looked at the young and even old who are under the curse of addiction.

The one that really caught my attention was a 20-year-old young man. Jewish!

He was held by a four-point restrain. I offered to sit with him so the Nurse could take a break and continue to complete her schedule.

He was very loud screaming Abba, Ruth and other names . . . . I had to close my ears with my finger to stop the deaf demonic sound coming from that young man.

Eventually, I spoke with him very calmly with a low, loving and gentle tone. He was calm. Then he began to share with me how his life had been.

He was born in Brooklyn, he has brothers and sisters, he explained how his mother had a difficult childbirth only with him and that the umbilical cord was tied around his neck.

He explained how close he was to death at birth. And how he grew up getting all the love from his parents, celebrated his Jewish tradition and attended college in Brooklyn.

And then went to Israel as soon as he graduated from college without telling his parents.

From the streets in Brooklyn he was always around many Caribbean youths and other cultures, he got hocked on drugs by following his college buddies and parting on weekends.

It was unbelievable that a Jewish man loved reggae or rap so much as he did. **Bob Marley, Tupac** and **Biggie Small** are just to name a few of his favorite's music artists.

For the time I spent with him I noticed how he responded to the Doctors, very aggressive, and my other co-workers, they even had to get security to accompany them into the room, they were afraid of him.

There I was with no fear, sitting in the room, talking with him and he even laughed.

I assisted him while I spoke with him by offering him some water to drink and clean his face, touch his arms, foot and checked for cyanosis.

The point is, I shared Jesus with him, he knew of Moses and tranquil the Jews wait for Jesus "Yeshiva", for the Messiah to come.

He was there all tied down and crying like a child, cursing and fighting, calling out for **Tupac, Biggie Small** and other raps artists names to help him.

I told him he is tied down in his heart also, so even when the restrains are removed he would be bound by his sins and he need to ask God to save him.

I began to share the word with him, "For God so Love the World that he gave his only begotten Son that whosoever believes in Him would not perish but have everlasting life".

Jesus was obedient to His father and went to the cross, shed his blood, and suffered the shame and pain to redeem us back to the father, Abba.

I told him it was never too late, and all he had to do is call on the name of Jesus and he would be delivered from the torment he feels.

I asked him how comes he believed in Moses, why can't he also believe in Jesus?

God had given Moses the Ten Commandments and Moses had others that he wrote for the people to stay healthy, and also that Jesus came and gave us new commandments.

"Love the Lord your God with all your Heart, soul, mind and strength and your neighbor as yourself".

When you read the Ten Commandments it seem so simple, but that is all we need to do just take God at his words.

Heaven and Earth will past away, but every word that was spoken by God through the messengers of God will come to past. Believe it or not!

The whole duty of man is to fear God and keep his commands. This is the whole purpose of our being here on this earth.

After all my talking with him, he began to sing, I felt it in my heart, I stood up and began to sing with him and then he fell asleep.

The Nurse told me he had not slept in two days; she came and removes the restrains.

They were amazed, he had not sleep so long and now he was sleeping peacefully. He was tormented, curing at the Doctors, the Nurses and anyone who came in the room to help him.

After a while he woke up I offered him food, the Nurses kept asking me what he said or what I talked with him about, he was calm again and walking around in the room.

Not long after that he walked out of the room, still calling out for Abba, not loudly this time but painfully.

I believe he was calling out for his biological father; Abba, they call and inform the staff that they had planned to come and see him the next day.

Even in the hallway everyone was getting out of the way and seems scared to have him close to them.

I went up to him and gently touch his arm and asked him to get back to bed, his mother and father will be there to see him.

This guy was so tall and big maybe he weigh over 200 pounds and was over 6 feet tall.

He was in bed all tied up so I had no idea how gigantic he really was, me with my petite 5"3", 150 pounds self and the grace of God, leading him back to his room.

I had experience God's power and I thank God in my heart for hearing my prayer. There is nothing too hard for God.

I really prayed for him then, that he would find peace and come to the knowledge of the saving grace of our Lord and savior Jesus Christ. "No man cometh to the father but by me" Jesus said.

I felt it deep in my soul, I really love people and I often prayed for them when I have to care for them (I still work in the hospital).

I often wondered, Lord, could I reach these people? Is it possible that they'll be saved even at this late time in their lives?

How is it possible that someone can live there entire life not experiencing God's love, God sent his Son to claim us, to get the keys of death and hell.

We had no way of getting back the love we lost, we were so sinful, look at all the things people are doing now, just think of the worst things a person can do, then think of the punishment.

God still love us, when we deserve to be doomed. How can you resist that love?

God's Love is Patient, his love never fails and he knows how the Spirit is working with and through us to cleanse our hearts until we are pure to enter his glory.

. . . In the last time there will be scoffers who will follow their own ungodly desires.

"There are the men who divide you who follow mere natural instincts and do not have the spirit, but you dear friends build yourselves up in your most Holy Faith and pray in the Holy Ghost, keep yourselves in Gods' love as you wait for the mercy of our Lord Jesus Christ to bring you into his glorious rest".

"Be merciful to those who doubt, snatch them out of the fire pit of hell and asked the Lord to save them". (Jude 1:18-22).

There is another friend of mine who was in a terrible situation. He was homeless at the time; he had been to jail, had no job and was very desolate.

I met him on the train a few months ago; God put people in our lives for different reasons, not personal but that they need you at the time.

We talk about his family, his faith and some bad experiences he has been through, I offer encouragement and told him to find a church to attend and to seek God and be more positive in his thinking.

I saw him the other day coming out of **Maggie Johnson Theatre**; he looked great, well dressed with a beautiful lady by his side, I felt so happy for him.

It does not matter how life looks now, just have faith and hold on for a little while longer and God will bring you through.

For me when I meet people I often look deep into their spirit, actually my spirit does that, I asked God to love them through me.

I often look for the God given gifts that maybe dominant in people as I talk with them.

Even the mention of the name of Jesus will touch my heart, if they could see the love of God in me, the pure love nothing missing, nothing broken and just God's grace.

I am a child of God, his servant. I have a mission and that is to seek and ask God to save, that which is lost, I am praying always for hurting people and the hopeless.

As Christians we had a job to absolute and that is to tell all we meet about the love of our father . . .

People see God as a sugar daddy; give me this give me that is that all you need from the almighty God, why can't you say Lord let your will be done in my life . . . .

If I never had a problem I wouldn't know God could solve it . . . . .

Often they say, "Well if God loves me why is my life in such a mess?" I asked God to open their spiritual eyes to see his glory; it is not about this life.

"If it is in this life we have hope we would be human (men) most miserable".

Then John the Baptist gave this testimony, "I saw the Spirit came down from heaven and remain on him, and the man on whom you see the spirit comes down and remain on is the one who will baptize with the Holy Spirit". (John1: 32-33).

And yet people are still looking for the Messiah? As Brother **Oral Roberts** says "The spirit walks beside us".

If God is in Heaven and Jesus is also sitting at his right hand, who is here on earth with us, to hear our every grooming?

Chapter 2

The Holy Spirit!

All of them were filled with the Holy Spirit and began to speak with other tongues as the spirit enabled them . . . Acts. 2: 4

In the last days, God said He will pour out his spirit on all people . . . . verse 17 so we all can experience that wonderful power, but I am glad I get to experience it now before the last day . . . .

My mind wonders to the computer where we enable some programs that are already in place . . .

The sensitivity is great, knowing we are never alone; you only can experience this "Cloud nine" by coming to the knowledge of our Lord and Savior Jesus Christ.

"You are witness to the things I am going to send you what my father has promised, but stay in the city until you have been clothed with power from on high". (Luke 24:48-49)

Jesus is Lord!

"Until the day he was taken up to heaven after giving instruction through the Holy Spirit to the Apostle he has chosen" . . . ."For John baptized with water, but in a few days you will be baptized with the Holy Spirit"

"You will receive power when the Holy Spirit comes on you" . . . . Acts 1: 2-5-8.

When the day of Pentecost came they were all together in one place, suddenly a sound like a blowing of a violent wind came from heaven and filled the whole house where they were sitting.

They saw what seems to be a tongue of fire that separated and came to rest on each of them.

All of the Disciples were filled with the Holy Spirit and began to speak in other languages as the spirit enabled them to do.

There were God-fearing Jews from every Nation under heaven. And when they heard this sound a crowd came together in bewilderment because each one heard them speaking in his own language . . . they made fun of them and said they have drank too much wine . . . Acts 2: 1-13

Even today people will motionlessly believe Christians are fanatical to speak in tongues.

The tongues of fire were for the physical eyes to see, something came over them. We have a gift. The world can see us regular people a good example is **Benny Hinn.**

He is a normal man yet we see how God is using him to show his power in healing and saving souls.

People are immobile with yearning for miracles, signs and wonders, such as fire coming down from heaven again.

Jesus prayed for the people who would believe through the words of the Bible, and from books today that are written by God-fearing people.

When you or a family member becomes ill or needs a miracle, have you even wondered how comes it became so easy to believe it would happen?

"Faith is the substance of things hope for the evidence of things not seen". Jesus healed people in his time and he said the same miracles that he did you would also do them and even greater.

Only believe all things are possible, "Greater is He (Holy Spirit) that is in us, than he (the devil) that is in the world".

When I am watching **Benny Hinn** Ministry and I see young people being healed, it brought me back to when I was a child and got healed.

God Heal children because he has a mission for them to do and who better able to talk about something than someone who have actual been in that situation?

If we see an adult healed we believe they are faking and someone must pay them off.

For children we sway a little but would believe it maybe real.

When I was about 14 years old, I had a lump in my breast that was so painful and very huge;

my mother got so scared and said she would take me to the Doctor the next day.

My grandmother (father's mom) died from breast cancer years again and now there I was. Even with all that pain my Grandmother, (Mother's mom) Mrs. Lydia, took me to her church that night.

And during the service the Pastor asked for people to come up for prayer and healing.

Mama asked me to go and let him pray for me, I did not hesitate but obey and went, I did not tell him what was wrong, but he anointed me with olive oil and prayed.

I went home, eat and went to sleep and in the morning, my mother told me to get dress she will be leaving for the Doctor by 9 a.m.

To my surprise there was no pain, no lump, oh my God I was healed, I jump and cried out "Mama there is no lump in my breast anymore", my mother said how can there be no lump, she explain how she felt it and know it was there, it can't just disappear.

I saw it with my own eye yesterday?

God had healed me!

A few years again when we came to New York and share the story with my sister, she told me she had several surgeries on her breast, and she even showed me the marks, breast cancer is in my father's family, but I plea the blood of Jesus to release my generation from that curse.

Wow.

The other miracle I experienced was my Uncle, Jim, (my mother's twin brother) he was so sick when he came back to visit, he was skinny and went to sleep, he had been away from home in Falmouth, Jamaica.

OMG, my mother got so scared and began to cry, did you come home to die? My mother cried so loudly all the neighbors came over to see what had happen.

"Oh, my brother is dying" she cried.

People from all over our small communities were running to our home, everyone saw him there lying on the bed. Jaundice was about to take his life.

My Grandmother (Mom's mother) called for some of her church people and they began to pray, to my surprise after maybe an hour, I heard a shout of joy, "he is alive he is OK"!

Jim got up off the bed and began to jump and speaking in tongues.

After many months my Uncle got a visa to Florida on farm work, he got married and had fours children.

He bought a large single-family house, taught himself to drive and worked until he died almost 15 years later, from some Heart ailment, or asthma. Some People in Florida live too far from the hospital.

My mother and my children went to see his family one Christmas, 1998 a year before he died, he cooked curry goat, green bananas and rice and peas, we had a big family re-union, my Uncle Ben and his wife and all of his wife's relatives attended church that week-end.

We went to the church and my mother talked to him about his life with God. My grandmother had thirteen children and she often prayed for all of them by name, even her grand children.

She really believed the Bible; she raised her children by waking them up 6 a.m. to pray and also 6 p.m. at night.

Each morning she prays with them and takes them to church with her each weekend, actually I think she went to church 5 days a week. She did the same with my brothers and sisters, she reads to us as small children and we read to her during our older years.

During that I memorized many verses in the Bible I could recite them as poems, I knew all the 66 books and could answer any question pertaining to the Bible.

Once when I was a teenager, my grandmother told me I spoke in tongues in my sleep.

I had memorized the Psalms and many Bible verses that I use in school yes; we had Religion in school.

I had a very weird child hood, my grandmother told us many ghost stories, guess she did not think of the mental aspect, I find it hard though, I had developed the spirit of fear, I was afraid of the dark, to be alone and just about anything.

I often fought with my cousin, Aldine, to accompany me to the store or school. I was on my way to school once; I saw a policeman and I ran back home.

My grandmother also told us a lot of stories about Jamaican folk's tale and "Spanish a jar" ghost stories. How could she know they would cause fear in a child, but it did in me.

We had no television, nor telephone so telling stories would be the way to go, she often spoke in tongues and talk with spirits, very weird.

One thing I realized during this was that our culture plays a great deal in molding us into who we are.

We trust God, he is good, he created the earth and we think he can't heal the sick, what kind of God we would serve?

Were we there when he sent his Son to die for the fallen race? Look at all the pain and agony Jesus went through, he said by His strips we are healed.

Just simple believe God's word.

When I think of how God has brought me this far, my mother told me she wanted to abort me, if you talk with many mothers today they would say the same thing.

I am one of them!

It was not in her power to do anything to me, God has a plan for my life, I have written many songs since my teenage years, sometimes I think I miss the opportunity but God knows why the delay.

God knows me and he loves me, though many childhood sickness, phobias, and lack. Crazy things, vision, and experiences once I even saw a ghost (you don't have to believe you can only talk about what you see) that is why I know the spirit is in me, I have a discerning spirit.

Often I really don't want to feel or see things around me but God is preparing me.

Even with my family, three of my children suffered from server Asthma, often in the hospital for two to three days, on medication and close monitoring.

One day after observing all the sickness, a voice said to me "don't you believe I can heal your children"? Wow!

Just then I took them one by one and began to pray, my son began to cough rigorously and after a while he up-trucked some black caviar looking stuff, and from that moment on, none of my children were sitting in any more emergency room with Asthma attack.

I had been baptized in the Holy Spirit at a teen's camp in Jamaica; it was a wonderful experience and still is. I am in love with Jesus.

You can experience this mostly during praying or singing praises and worship songs. I love the way the spirit moves, I realize I am a spirit living in a body!

After each experience with God I am calm and relax. "You will fill me with joy in your presence".

Chapter 3

"In his presence that's where I belong, in his presence, Oh Lord my God". I am strong in your presence. "In the last days", God says," I will pour out my spirit on all people". (Acts 2: 17).

Why wait for the last minute to trust in God, life is not cut smooth and dry? If you are on your deathbed and you won the lottery, one million dollars. That is great but how can you enjoy the money? You are on your way home . . . out!

I believe now is the time to enjoy God riches on the earth while you have the strength and senses.

Now is the time to be filled with the Holy Spirit. Enjoy the gifts now while you have life, why live in pain, when God said by his strips you are healed?

Desolation and grief when God says, I will never leave you or forsake you!

Sin is sweet . . . Trust me I know, because all have sinned and come short of the glory of God.

Don't forget the wages of sin is death, eternal separation from God, can you imagine having a day without the sun shining or the wind blowing?

The gift of God is eternal life!

Peace and joy, love everlasting and the peace that passes all understanding, tell me one sin that is in your life, which is so good, that you would rather died and go to hell than give it up?

All these years all you have encountered was pain, suffering and desolation, can you allow one thing to control your life so much that you become a robot. Will it cause you your life? Yes!

Is it your friends, you can find new ones in God's family. Think about what God had done through Jesus on the cross to save a loss world.

There are seven continents, trillions of people, who will hold your hands in hell, who will hear your anguishing pain on your deathbed?

Even now in this world sin seems to be dominating between the devil and sin.

You see how this gay life style is taken over our world; often we get scared and wonder what will happen to the next generation?

Listen to me; let not your heart be troubled, God is still in control, have you forgotten what happen in the era of Sodom?

It got so bad that even when the Angels came to take Lot and his family out of Sodom, they were overcame by those men who refused to even have virgins.

So often I saw these men who claimed to be gay walking with a beautiful woman, **Tyra** and her friends, I just laugh, the Bible cannot be wrong, they are left up to their reprobate minds, they lost the desire for women.

We still have to preach to them, show them love and let them know that we all have sinned, but we need to stop and allow God to live in us.

We are not just on this earth to live, have sex, and then die. There has to be more, we were created for a purpose.

Look at men of old, Paul, Peter and Moses. God need our hands, we are concern that we need to change who we are, a man wants to be a woman, paying thousand of dollars to do body enhancements. Get a hobby; go feed the poor in a third world country.

Children in other part of the world dying for food, the basic needs and here you are affluently living. Just love you and focus on helping someone else.

Even here in New York City, I did not know that people could sleep on floor with their children, until when I was homeless.

There is so much work to do; it is not all about us. Someone needs your help.

If your trust God you don't have to live in fear anymore, God has to key of death, no need to fear it, "Oh grave where is that victory or death where is thy sting?"

I often overheard people talking about all the evil in the world, and asked where God is in all this? They say the Pastors all want to get rich and don't help the church people, but listen to me let them get rich, they are enjoying their earthy life what are you doing to fulfill your gifts and talents?

Don't waste your precious life worrying about others, live your own life. Wheat and tares will grow until the day of harvest; we are not the judges of others!

Promotion comes from God and he gives us knowledge how to gain wealth, what we do after that it is up to us. The secret of the Lord is with them that love him and are called according to his purpose.

God will prosper you if you are faithful to his words, fear God and keep his commandments!

The race is not for the swift or the battle for the strong but for those that endure to the end.

With all this world's wealth, resources and technology, it still does not appear, or even our mind can conceive all the blessings that God has in store for all that love him. You can be blessed in this life!

We are people who have many issues and life struggles, we all have fears, and we need love and security. Seek the biggest source. God!

Jesus was just a prophet?

"I can tell you confidently that the patriarch David died and was buried and his tomb is here" . . . ."He was not abandoned to the grave nor does his body see decay. God has raised Jesus to life and we are all witness of the fact". Act 2:29

The father promised when Jesus leaves He would send the comforter the Holy Spirit. Exalted to the right hand of God, He had received from the father the promised Holy Spirit and has poured out what you now see and hear. Act 2:33.

We as believers have oneness with the Holy Spirit; often I woke up at 5:45 a.m. with a song in my heart, I also felt the presence of the Holy Spirit.

(I miss my time with you, often if I wake and forget to pray I feel terrible during the entire day).

I have my devotion and listen to the broadcast every morning from 5:30 on channel 9 **(O'Dollar, Hinn and Copeland)**. It is so much easier to start my day with God praises on my lips. The other soul feeding is **WBLS 1190** a.m. Sister Yolanda . . .

"Everyone was filled with awe followed by many wonders and miraculous signs that were done by the apostles (44)".

"Stretch out your hand to heal and perform miraculous signs and wonders through the name of your holy Savior Jesus".

"And they were all filled with the Holy Spirit and spoke the words of God boldly". Act 4:30-32.

This is our technology era and many people are still set on "Show me some proof". Do they want Jesus to be born again?

(Humor) Here, His parents in Manhattan atone of those plash Plazas or The Trump Tower, guess he could be born in Central Park and grow up in the Bronx, "Can anything good comes from the Bronx". The Bronx 2008 will be great!

Where will we find a Calvary or we could put him on death roll at Rockers' Island.

We have lots of Jews in Brooklyn; some still don't believe he came already. Get on with the doubts!

The man came, lived, died and is in Heaven interceding for us at the right hand of God. What is there for you not to believe, what do you have to lose . . . your soul? Believe in the Lord Jesus Christ and you will be saved.

Our proof is here on earth the Holy Spirit has bore the witness.

Why is your heart so hard? You don't want to give up sin in your life. Well don't! The wages of sin is death, eternal separation from God.

Come with your heavy load, come as you are, you can't change a thing in your life along!

If you have no new clothes, come if you have no money, well walk to a closes church, there are so many Churches on the corners in this city, do anything to hear the words of God!

The Church people may not be what you expect; some of us believe "happily ever after", the church is a body of believer who gather together to strengthen each other, "iron sharpens iron".

Many Churches feed people, clothes and even help with other expenses, we need each other, "no man is an Island, no man stands along each one joy is joy to me each man brief is my own". Big up **LGA**!

One thing I have learned over the years is that, if you want friends you have to make friends, get people telephone numbers, talk to people and do things together.

You can't live and just pretend all is well, and bit your teeth pretending we are not in pain. Call on God!

Then Peter said, "Ananias how is it that Satan has so filled your heart that you have lied to the Holy Spirit and have kept for yourself some of the money you received for the land"? Act 5:3

Who get to lead Gods' people?

I have spoken to people and many times all their reply would be "the Pastors are taken all the poor people money and living large".

You see in those days the money was for all the people, no one was poor or homeless.

One of my favorite Pastors is Dr. **Creflo**, this is funny, I heard him preaching once and he said people said he change his name to Dollar, he said, " why would I want to be call Dollar when I could be called a millionaire"?

I will always support his Minister, I am glad God has used another black man, because we can relate when he spoke of his upbringing and childhood challenges.

My only son will have a role model . . . . big up our first African American President, **Obama!**

Dr. Dollar has a real testimony, God is no respect of people, He can use anyone, it is time to stop judging the man of God and find your own purpose.

He did what God placed in his heart, what we have to lose, our self; we have too much to gain to lose.

Often when I try to witness to people about the goodness of the God we serve and to follow his examples, by doing good and caring for people, only to be cut off by a load of negative words about these new age preachers and the church people this and that . . . .

How do one justify and help them to see that God's people are blessed and men gives unto us, gifts pressing down, shaken up and running over.

You can't hate them just pray to God, "**Lord bless me and enlarge my territory**". I know what it feels like when someone asks you for money and you don't have it.

TV, ministers are always asking for money . . . . . .

"Brothers choose seven men from among you who are known to be full of the Holy Spirit and wisdom". Act 6:3

When we obey the Spirit the church will begin to grow and prosper. Shalom.

"You stiff necked people with uncircumcised hearts and ears you are just like your father you always resist the Holy Spirit". Act 7:51

This makes me wonder how will my children love God, I heard a Pastor says, "great men praise God and live a good life but when they die their children becomes rebellions and turn away from God words".

As much as the time changes and people seem so far from God, he is God and He is the Alpha and Omega.

God can never lose!

This is a tragic! Serving God for years and still has not received the Holy Spirit.

"When they arrived (Peter and John) they prayed for them that they might receive the Holy Spirit, because the Holy Spirit had not yet come upon them, they have simply been baptized into the name of the Lord Jesus, then Peter and John placed their hands on them and they receive the Holy Spirit". Acts 8:15-19

Simon tried to purchase the gift, even as I write my thoughts went back to Pastor Benny Hinn. We see no powerful action on his part, all he does is pray or lay his hands and God does the rest, through the Holy Spirit.

He only needs a body, our bodies, our voice and obedience to reach human in today's society.

Man can touch the outer body, physically that is all we can see, but spiritually the work is complete inside.

A Title I chose after many topics, the reason is how God has worked in my life over the years, the many experiences I had and now be able to look back and say, wow, all I had to do was " let go"!

One experience, I was late for work, I leave normally before 10:00 pm. To get there by 11:00 p.m, (I work the grave yard shift, not by my own intent but I believe God has a reason for everything and we have to be obedient).

I got so scared, suddenly it dawned on me that I had no money to get to work, and I could not drive at night with my learners' permit all the way to 14th. Street.

I called the first person whom to help me that late, and ask him to come and take me to work, or give me some money to purchase a metro card.

I had to leave the house right away, I had no time to explain why I had no money, I got so frustrated, and left the house, no change to call in the train station and let someone at my job know I was on my way . . .

I hold on to the promise that I will never be broke another day in my life, how good is it to have all your money in the bank and can't get it that late . . . anyway.

Wow, tight spot! I went to the train station and pull out my card thinking I had no money on it, but then to my surprise there was $7.00.

I swiped and went in, and then I thought what about calling work? I search through my bag, pennies but no quarters.

I asked the first lady who passed me, "Can you change these for a whole quarter"? She refused; and then a man came behind her, heard me ask and offered me one quarter to make the call.

I smile to myself and told him thanks and made the call. I trust God!

Often we are place with our back against the wall, the first thing we face is fear, but God will always provide.

Obedience

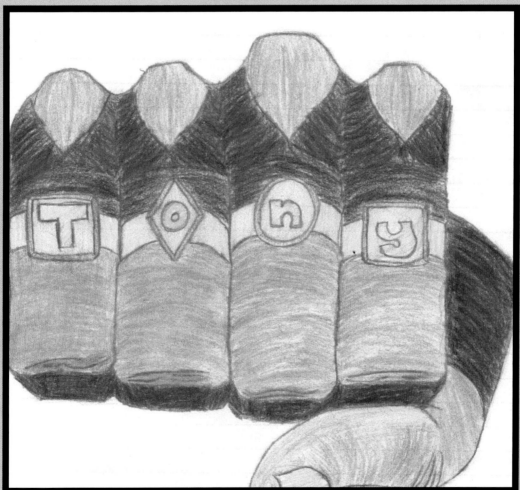

This has been my challenge from a child and I realized this set me back a great deal, when we are disobedient to our parents it follows throughout our lives in all our major discussions.

I have not obeyed the Holy Spirit on many occasions; you see it is a still small voice that you can choose to ignore.

I am enrolled in College and now I change my mind and am wondering do I belong here? With the entire lecture about HMO, Medical Care, making lots of money and clever ways to increase our income, I want to win souls for God or help people not rip someone off to get rich.

My grandmother died and as I talked with my Uncle and he wanted me to send some money to help with the funeral. I am thinking it would be a great idea to send it with my father; I won't be able to make the trip at this time.

Making lots of money is always the norm; it is 1.a.m. in the morning I started to cry, this is June 21, 2006.

I can't go to the funeral, my grandmother raised me, she was very sick and now she is dead.

I am not crying because she is death but I did not get to see her before and I have extra money saved for this occasion, but was still on probation at this new job.

My prayer at this time was "Lord what kind of life is this, I need to start living my best life, and all I am now is exiting.

Thank you Lord for changing my life, I have let go!

Well, let me make the best of this, so I send the money, made a cassette with a song I wrote along with a letter explaining how sorry I was to miss the funeral.

I got a video from the funeral, the nine nights, (wake) and the great celebration at the funeral, wow, my heart was please.

I know my grandmother was prosperous, all the ministers, the people from our community and many guests.

God did not create any junk, he makes us wonderful and beautiful, I am a gold mine with all the songs I wrote, the poem and my skills.

Fear has prevented me from reaching my full potential. I need to live for God, open my understanding, please deliver me from the sneers of the enemy, I have your words in my heart I have faith, so what is preventing me from excelling in my dream?

Break through; now, set my mind, my body and my soul free. I can do it I know God is for me; I am tired of being indigent, enough already.

Then Ananias (Maybe the same one that later died from keeping the money) went to the house and enter it, placing his hands on Saul, he said, "Brother Saul, the Lord Jesus who appear to you has sent me so that you may see again and be filled with the Holy Spirit . . ."

Usually one gets save, baptized and then filled with the Holy Spirit. That's how it was for me.

I received the gift then and gave my life to God. I did not know much about all the things God did for us; such as sending his Son to die on a cross, suffer shame and desolation.

Jesus came so I can live, I wanted to live; I did not want to go to Hell. What did the devil do for me?

This experience came from a Movie "Pilgrim Progress" our church had a movie night on the lawn and on a large projector in the Churchyard we gathered to watch.

At that time I must have been about 12 or 13 years old, but from my grandmother's teaching it all made sense as I began to really understand what Jesus did when he died on that cross.

I cried, I really emptied my heart and asked Jesus to come into my heart and save me; soon after that while attending a summer youth camp, I got filled with the Holy Spirit in my teens.

And to be filled was the greatest feeling I could ever experienced. Even now in my late 30s, I am still in love with Jesus.

People often believe we were already born with the gifts of the Holy Spirit. "You will receive power after the Holy Ghost" and why did Peter ask those believers, have they received the Holy Spirit since you believe?

Many people fake it, you either have it or you don't, get some soul spiritual music and go into your room and begin to pray, even if it takes all day, it is vital to have a real power working within you.

As I listen to Creflo today, he spoke about children of God and of the devil and you know from talking to some people that you need not ask who is your daddy, whose children are you, man you can feel that spirit.

Pastor Benny spoke of when he was a child, and even for many of us who grew up in very strict home, where we cannot wear or say anything that comes to our mouth.

The way people live has to change, many of us gave our lives to Christ very early, it is not easy but the main thing is to have God in your life.

God is a spirit and they that worship him MUST worship in spirit and truth.

We were all born in sin, and then we are born again when we receive Christ as our savior.

He gives us gifts, Love, Joy, Peace, longsuffering, temperance and many others we see manifested in our lives each day.

Just as Paul's (Saul the Christian persecutor) eyes were blinded, we were born blind until Jesus saves our soul, but we have to ask him to come in.

"Behold I stand at the door and knock if anyone will open, I will come in and dine with him".

When we tap into the gifts that we receive when we accept Jesus into our heart, we feel the joy, the peace and love that reaches deep into our souls.

I worked in a Nursing Home and I can't understand how these people are on their way out (death bed) and they still have no need for God.

I try or do my best to share the love of God, but they often asked me if I really believed all that stuff or someone told me.

Yes, someone did! My Grandmother, who died a few months again, she often takes me to church with her, she reads the words of God with me and told me all about the love of God and not just by words of her mouth, but by her example and my own knowledge after studying the scriptures for myself.

What else could I live by, I never smoke, drink or do drugs, how else could I get high, but on God, I tell you if you never experienced the Holy Ghost high you can't see what I am talking about.

One very experience I had, I was so depressed and frustrated and I went to church, there I was praying and felt all burdened down, then a sister came and prayed with me, I began to sing and get in tuned with my spirit, wow.

All my burdens were gone, when I left the church, I felt so refreshed and light, and from that day I can say God has lifted me.

No matter the situation there is only one person to turn to, and that is God. You know when you are alone, all the things you have to struggle with, so you have to go to God alone and in private and he will always see you through.

Thanks be to God, my grandmother see the need to allow me to experience the love of God, and did not say, "Well, when you are older or when you understand".

People can be very selfish and doesn't care for each other; we have to leave it to God, not taken it personally.

Only God can care for you the way you deserve, love you the way you deserve and understands you, really understands you.

It is great to let the teaching of the older folks process our cognitive. Look at the prize that we will be facing after death, HELL or HEAVEN is there really a choice? In this world who tries to live a life of pain, and anguish? Everyone wants love, peace and joy.

I have a heart for God's people.

I could spend hours taking to someone who desires to know more about God, my evangelism at work, secondly, the gift of Hospitality, I love to serve others and enjoy seeing them happy.

As soon as an individual comes around me, all I am thinking is what can I do or give to make your life more pleasant.

First, for people on the streets who can benefit from my presence here on this earth, if they ask me for money, my motto is "God provides seed for the sewer", therefore, if I have it you got it.

A great way I see to help someone is with my Metro card!

Often it seems so small but people need to get around this city and often we don't have a penny.

God will place people in our path to help us, I am one of them and often I also need help.

God has brought me a might long way and I believe with all my heart he will take me all the way.

"The promise of a Land flowing with Milk and Honey".

For a young girl coming to this country with no idea of what to do with her life, twice homelessness, a fail marriage, with four children, often impecunious, welfare, and then getting the chance to attend two Colleges (**Monroe and Lehman**) completed my Bachelor in Business and now at one of the Best Hospital in **New York City. Beth Israel Medical Center** . . .

When I look back over my life, it is hard to believe that I had a father here and went through all this life of pain, it was known to him and it did not matter.

I do love my Dad, but I had another father who told me he will never leave or forsake me, I could trust him with my life, no matter what life place, regurgitate or obstacles my part.

It was all to glorify and prove to others who God, the lover of my soul, really is, for anyone who feels the hurt of not having that earthy father standing by your side, let go of the hurt and frustration.

The God who is always on time will be there for eternity!

Wow, so good my heavenly father is like that, He cares enough to supply your fundamental needs.

As I look over these notes especially that last line it sound so much as Paul when he was writing to the churches about his experiences, in jail, ship wreck and desolate.

Who knows what tomorrow may brings, one thing I know God is in my tomorrow. And I can go on . . . . **Celine Dion** . . . . My heart will go one . . . .

You also can trust him with your life . . . often we are strong and healthy so we don't need a savior, but try living your life without calling on God . . . Everyone does sometime of other . . .

"Oh my God".

Yes, he is our God and he is good, many have testified to the fact, please trust and obey God, we were created for a purpose, please don't let this moment pass you by.

Pray with me . . . **Father God in the name of Jesus, I need you to come into my heart and teach me how to trust you each day . . . . open my eyes, my mind and my heart to see your goodness and know you are real, Lord come into my heart I need you today . . . Amen . . . .**

Find a church and meet with people . . . . please don't say church people are impostures! God alone knows our heart, give them a chance . . .

I love you and God loves you best . . . For God so love the world that he gave his only begotten Son that **whosoever** believes in him will not perish, but have everlasting life . . . For God sent not His Son into the world to condemn you . . . . God loves you!

I was sharing with my daughter, Tashel, how God has given us the spirit of power and a sound mind . . . and this is the time that I really got the meaning.

For God has not given us the spirit of fear but of love, power and a sound mind.

I had a real big problem with fear as a child and it manifested itself in my adult life.

I have overcome the spirit of fear to an extent but I never claimed my sound mind. The power we got is to gain wealth and still a lot of things are missing in our lives.

We have to take these things by force; it is so good to trust God because everyday there are new mercy and meaning for life.

I am taking my mind back, my fear has to go and I will gain the wealth, God wants "Shalom" for his children, nothing missing, nothing broken, we walk in good health and peace each day.

I refuse to allow my life to be missing out on all the blessings God has in store for my family and the people he place in my path.

We need to know God is our father, Abba, and "no good thing will be withhold from them that walk upright", do good for people, love and give not expecting anything in return.

I claim my peace in the name of Jesus, and you should also . . . . God is good!

In our church we started the book "**Emotionally Healthy Church**" this is my second time around, a lot of the emotions had gone over the years, but we are still under construction and

God is not finish with us yet.

Often people look at church people and thought that they should have it together once they are baptized, filled with the Holy Spirit and are saved.

We can make it even though it seems so hard, our back is against the wall, our faith is failing and our strength is almost gone.

Let go and let God.

Who created you? Are you here and this earth because you wanted to be here?

Often when I am tempted to worry about my children, I just breathe a word of prayer and say "Lord you created them for your purpose therefore I place them in your care".

Life is getting real tense; everyone has an opinion on right and wrong. Why are you wasting your energy?

We need answer there is only one place to find that and it is in the Bible . . . . every challenges you face in life, any questions you may have the answers are there.

Even the question about if God loves Gay people . . . . 1 Corinthians 6: 9-20!

. . . . "Do you not know the wicked will not inherit the kingdom of God?

"Do not be deceived; neither the sexually immortal not idolaters nor adulteress nor male prostitutes nor homosexual will inherit the kingdom of God" . . . . . "but you are washed" . . . "and were justified in the name of Lord Jesus Christ" . . . "flee from sexual immorality" . . . . "all sin a man commit is outside his body" . . . "the body is temple of the Holy Spirit" . . . "you are not your own" . . . "therefore honor God with your body".

You would be surprise when you find all these things in the Bible . . . but trust me they are all there.

"Be still and know that He is God; he will be exalted over the whole earth". The world is changing so fast but, "be still and know that God is God and he will be exalted over the whole earth".

At **Love Gospel Assembly,** we are experiencing the blessings of God; we just had our 37th Anniversary and a banquet at the Bronx Botanical Gardens.

The **Promise Land Project**!

Now we are working on our emotional aspect, we all have been through things and we became ashamed and hide them, we talked about sharing secrets in one of our Sunday School Sessions.

Why do we keep secrets? Well, they are secrets, but why keep them and let it become like a barrier that held us captive?

Many times we keep secret from our family and friends, for example my daughter found my book and read the things I did.

People believe when you are a Christian there are some guidelines and you dear not cross them.

God said, "My yoke is easy and my burden is light".

I have done some things that I would not just go to my church family and confess it, and I guess when I keep it then it became my secret.

If I told them it would have been over and done, well, the devil made me do it . . . . .

Therefore, I will find ways of telling it, after God had forgiven me. One really bad thing that the enemy caught me with was an abortion.

When I got pregnant the first time I thought the world fell on me, how will my church people see me now?

There I was even at twenty one years old, motionless thinking like a teenager.

And I plan on having an abortion, my thoughts were no one will know, but then the Holy Spirit convicted me that He would know.

And I choose to carry the gift God has place in my care.

I am praying that God will not allow this generational curse to follow my family even with all that conviction of living right, the enemy still got me.

I got marry had two other children and then the enemy raise his head, "girl you are having too many children and they are so close together", and with many problems in my marriage I chose to have one between Tashel and Rose.

I believe in life and I know God has forgiving me.

Now when I look at my children it made me think what if?

"He without sin cast the first stone".

All have sinned and come short of the glory of God, we thrive to please God and live amiss the enemy stubborn attack we press on in Jesus name.

I imagine things happen in our lives to keep us humble, and therefore, we cannot condemn each other; because all sin is sin, no big sin or little sin, just sin!

We know living this life is not a rose garden, living in the real world cause us guilt and shame but God is merciful and full of compassion.

He loves us when we were sinners and cared nothing about him. God loves you and wants to make it right, He alone is righteous.

God is merciful and will give me the courage to live in a world of sin; Jesus prayed that the father would keep us in this world.

In my walk and sharing the goodness of God with others and telling them how God can wash away all our guilt and shame.

I was sharing that the Muslim believes they are going to heaven to get seven virgins.

We are spirit who lives in a body, when we die where someone will get a body to have relationship, "**I did not have relation with that woman**", we are neither male nor female, and we are all spiritual beings in the spiritual realm.

We will all be there to praise and glorify the father, who has redeemed us out of the hands of the evil one . . .

One of my other secrets was having a Muslim man in my life for seven years.

I spoke to two of my Pastors and they prayed with me about it, I still did not want to let it go, then I went to an all night prayer meeting and I prayed that God will give me the courage to get out of this relationship that is not pleasing in his sight.

You may ask how it is not pleasing. For one, because every time I spoke to this guy about faith in God, it was like talking to a brick wall.

I was always in such a rage and my spirit was always uneasy. Remember we are spirit and we live in a body.

My spirit was perturbed.

I always look at him and wonder how it can be that I cannot let this guy in my heart, he is handsome and looks great, but something in me could not let him in . . . .

Life Struggles.

One of my prayers was," Lord please don't let me make discussions now that will block my future with you, I love you too much".

God is concern about every area of our lives, he knows us when we were in our mother's womb and he will never leave us or forsakes us, no matter how rebellious and sinful we may get, and there is always mercy.

God will forgive, all we have to do is acknowledge him and he will direct our path.

Chapter 4

Picture By: Rosemarie

This is from a conversation I had with "Mr. Muslim man . . . . .

Women have no equal share in their world, submission can be cool but how can an educated woman who understood the world around her, completely surrender her life to a man for him to tell her how to dress, talk and act?

We have done that for God, not for a mare man!

She needs more out of life than just sitting at home waiting for a man to give her a few dollars, and then you have to explain how each dime is spent.

I asked him, "Are we going to live in a separate heaven or women will all turn into males?

How can a God who created male and female not love us equally?

What's with the separation!

Now you see why having an unequal yoke marriage or relationship is difficult. There are always contradictions or the need to explain situations; we have so many problems why take on such a severe one to live with for life?

God made two people, Adam and Eve, be fruitful and multiple, but our world has change with religion, culture and language and it will take the grace of God to live and have a healthy life, mentally and physically.

There are so many contradictions in this world but stay focus and let the Holy Spirit lead and guide your every step.

"The more I know your power Lord, the more I am mindful of how casually we speak or say your name".

Lord we praise your Holy name.

I will not be push around and be treated as a stranger in the house of my father.

This was October 10, 2005, I went to Dr. **Creflo Dollar** service at **Madison Square Garden**, we were the first in line to get in the theater, and we waited almost two hours to get in.

My children and I waited in the rain and it was cold and they were very miserable and wanted to go home.

"Mom can we go now"?

I forced them to stay and promise it will be a great experience, as everyone went in and began to choose their seats we also choose some seats close to the front.

There were almost twenty people therefore we had the choices among the seats.

An usher came over to us and told us we could not sit there, we had to sit in the back, so we went to the second section and sat.

Just then another lady came over and said we cannot sit here.

"Oh my God", not here not now, this is a place of worship and the devil coming to mess with me.

I asked her, "Where should we sit?

She offered, "somewhere over in the back". Are you kidding me?

Hell no, I am not moving; we wouldn't be able to see Dr. Dollar, in person.

I looked at my tired children, the place was empty and you want me to sit where?

I guess we were not dress in suits of white.

In a place of worship, I bit my lip, because things like this make a Christian curse.

Now as I stood to pray with the other people, my eyes were close and to my surprise.

Another lady came and touches me and asked me to move, this is the church policy children cannot sit so close to the camera.

I open my eyes to see the greeter, I just simple say, "OK we will be leaving soon".

Oh my God, this is a theater not even a real church, how can I praise God now.

While, all around me people were praying in tongues and singing praises to God.

And there I was now upset and very angry.

All I could do now was to stood still and say nothing, this is suppose to be people who love God, but I was not dress the part, or look like I have money, therefore let her sit in the back.

You see that is why when I go to church and they told me to sit in the back I feel so rejected and outcast.

Even in the Bible you see how they would treat people who are dress in gold or rich outfits.

This not to be in God's house, it is not all about how you look.

Jesus said come unto me as you are, God will change you in time . . .

People have to be famous, before they can be treated as human; I love to be in church so you can imagine how many times this happening to me.

In God's house you better purchase a chair; I will thrive to be great in my father's house.

I assisted in children church, I dance with Devotion in Motion, still I have not reach my full potential to what God created me to do, I just know there is something else I should be doing.

I feel in my spirit that there are many tasks, gifts we have not tap into, so many talents. (Writing, singing, caring, loving and service)

As long as I am silent I will be frustrated, we were all given the power when the Holy Ghost came, so I need to be out there, go into the entire world . . . .

Thanks be to God for the church.

Can I call a person on the street and say let me pray with you?

I can do that in church!

They would just keep on walking; I have tried this with an old lady who was in a wheelchair.

I was sharing how God could heal not just her body but her mind and save her soul.

Then I offered to pray with her and she just did not want to have me pray with her in public.

Where else we can speak in tongues, only at the church or in our homes. People would just call the police.

Crazy people!

We have a voice and thanks be to God we can be at liberty in the house of God.

It does not matter what the devil do or try to use people in the house, he also have his workers in there to distract or disappoint you.

He will never get me to stop attending and be apart of the service.

I have gone through "**40 Days of Purpose**", now we are doing much more studies on giving to God's work.

Building a promise Land Project.

My abilities have been stirred up and I will never be the same again, Praise God!

"May the Lord bless you and keep you, may the Lord show you his kindness, may He have mercy on you, may the Lord watch over you, and gives you peace". Number 16:24-26

"Cast all your cares upon the Lord because He cares for you". 1 Peter 5:7

Matthew 11:28, "Come unto me all he that labor and are heavy leaden and He will give you rest".

1 John 1:9, " . . . But if we confess our sins, he will forgive us our sins". We can trust God He does what is right. He will make us clean from all the wrong we have done".

"We have trouble all around us, but we are not defeated, we do not know what to do, but we do not give up" . . . 2 Corinthians 4:8.

"In all thy ways acknowledge him and he will direct thy path . . . .".

Lucy and I at our gala

Gala ..President I. and few college buds...

Get down with your bad selves . . . .

Teacher Aide, NYC 2004,

Bronx Charter School.

After graduating high school first job as a Teacher Aide . . . .

Davyton Basic School. Desreen, Dawn and Me.

Yes, a brides made, my Uncle Ashton's wedding.

My brother, Paul's wedding: back, niece Kathy, nephew Paul, daughter Rose, me, daughter Tiffani, niece Kathleen and daughter Tashel. (TJ hiding in the back) Front, dad Keith, sister—in—law Loraine, Brother Paul, and mother Rose.

Cousin, Aldine and his wife.

The Pastor and Pam by the door.

Daughter Tiffani, me, Tashel, Rose and Kathleen and Paul's head.

Art work by Tony (my son age 14)

Printed in the United States
by Baker & Taylor Publisher Services